TOP CLASS

Grammar

Year 3

Now supported with CPD training
For info visit www.johnmurraycpd.co.uk

John Murray

Published by Hopscotch, a division of MA Education, St Jude's Church, Dulwich Road, London, SE24 0PB
www.hopscotchbooks.com
020 7738 5454

©2017 MA Education Ltd

Written by John Murray

Series designed by Claire Swaffield, Fonthill Creative, 01722 717029

Cover illustration by Sara Anderton
www.catandfoxadventures.com

Associate Publisher: Angela Morano Shaw

ISBN 9781909860094

All rights reserved. This resource is sold subject to the condition that it shall not, by way of trade or otherwise, be lent, hired out or otherwise circulated without the publisher's prior consent in any form of binding or cover other than that in which it is published and without a similar condition, including this condition, being imposed upon the subsequent purchaser.

No part of this publication may be reproduced, stored in a retrieval system, or transmitted, in any form or by any means, electronic, mechanical, photocopying, recording or otherwise, without the prior permission of the publisher, except where photocopying for educational purposes within the school or other educational establishment that has purchased this book is expressly permitted in the text.

Every effort has been made to trace the owners of copyright of material in this book and the publisher apologises for any inadvertent omissions. Any persons claiming copyright for any material should contact the publisher who will be happy to pay the permission fees agreed between them and who will amend the information in this book on any subsequent reprint.

Contents Page

Introduction _____ 6

Plurals _____ 8

Proper Nouns _____ 12

Pronouns _____ 16

Verbs _____ 20

Modal Verbs _____ 24

Adverbs _____ 28

Adjectives _____ 32

Conjunctions _____ 36

Present Continuous _____ 40

Past Continuous _____ 44

The Infinitive _____ 48

Past Simple I _____ 52

Past Simple II _____ 56

The Past Perfect _____ 60

Introduction

Top Class is a series that endeavours to combine traditional approaches to the teaching and learning of grammar, punctuation and vocabulary with new techniques and activities that support and encourage good learning.

The three core areas have been separated into three distinct books aimed primarily at Key Stage 2. The three books ought to be used in conjunction with each other in order to provide learners with a wider learning environment and for them to understand that these core elements of Literacy work together and are not to be applied in isolation.

Specific elements of the new Key Stage 3 National Curriculum have also been included in order to introduce Key Stage 2 learners to more complex grammatical constructions and vocabulary as they make their transition from attaining National Standard to Mastery.

Each book, one for each Year group in Key Stage 2, aims to promote discussion about specific areas of Literacy and provides experiences and opportunities to use and apply what they have learnt.

The three books are as follows:

- Top Class – Grammar
- Top Class – Punctuation
- Top Class – Vocabulary

Each book contains lessons that develop a 'top-down' approach, allowing learners to see how we use language in context, not simply *when* we use a particular word, punctuation mark or grammatical construct but *how* to use it to its best effect when writing independently.

As such, it actively promotes the core principle that to learn grammar and punctuation well and to extend your personal vocabulary effectively, then you must not only see these particular elements of Literacy within authentic and meaningful context and settings but you must then have the opportunity to apply what you have understood in your own independent writing.

All too often children are taught grammar, punctuation and vocabulary with exercises that aren't rooted within an authentic experience; and, as a result, although they may gain full marks in their exercise books, they often misapply or omit what has been learnt in their own free writing.

The *Top Class* series seeks to address this problem using a three staged approach, each Lesson Plan being structured so that learners are encouraged to investigate and explore the English language; initially with support and guidance from their teacher and fellow peers before being asked to apply what they have learnt as individuals.

Think about...

Before undertaking the Guided activity, learners are asked about what they already know about a particular piece of punctuation or grammatical form and where they might have seen it.

This links directly to the Guided text, again helping learners to view grammar, punctuation and vocabulary in context, housing it so that stronger links can be made with prior learning and personal experiences. This can then be used as a springboard to explore and develop this further in a familiar setting.

For example, when looking at our use of capital letters when writing a proper noun, learners may be asked about why people use an atlas or map before looking at a tourist map of London and considering why place names and famous tourist attractions start with a capital letter.

Guided

This is a shared activity that engages the whole class.

Set within a specific and relevant genre of Literacy, it embeds each particular piece of grammar, punctuation or vocabulary being taught in a focused and meaningful way. Moreover, it invites learners to use this information in order to answer a series of questions that are related to the text itself and then begins to move beyond it.

Each of the three questions asked have been carefully formatted so that valuable practice for the end of *Key Stage 2 English grammar, punctuation and spelling test* can be undertaken throughout each Year group. Marks are also available so that pupils gain practice at providing fuller explanations for those questions where two or three marks are being awarded. Answers are provided on the Lesson Plan.

Independent

This activity can be completed as an individual, with a partner or within a small group.

Each Independent activity within the book is also differentiated at an upper and lower level* and offers teachers a range of practical activities that support learners as they practise what they have learnt in the Guided section.

Differentiated activities can be found on the CD Rom.

Homework

Included in this section is a homework activity that aims to encourage wider learning outside of the classroom to take place. There are two types of homework activities that are provided, each having been designed to help learners discover and engage with grammar, punctuation and vocabulary in the 'real' world:

A] Specific 'closed' questions may be asked in order that research skills, both modern and traditional, can be employed to find a particular answer.

For example: What is the capital city of Denmark? Who was the first man to walk on the moon? When necessary, answers are provided on the Lesson Plan.

B] Wider 'open' tasks are given in order to afford learners the opportunity to explore the world around them and collect examples that are both pertinent and authentic.

For example, learners may be asked to find three examples where a shop's name uses an **apostrophe in their local high street**.

Extension

This final stage of the learning journey is an important one and underscores the importance of using a 'top-down' approach to the teaching and learning of grammar, punctuation and vocabulary.

Each Extension activity within the book is also differentiated at an upper and lower level.*

Its aim is to encourage children to apply what they have learnt in a meaningful and purposeful way in order to embed their learning.

For example, learners may be asked to write a shopping list when planning a party that will naturally include a colon or use strong adjectives to describe a certain event in a story.

More importantly, it is this *writing for purpose* (rather than to score arbitrary marks or achieve irrelevant ticks in an exercise book) that provides a meaningful opportunity for individuals to engage with the English language and create their own work that uses grammar, punctuation and vocabulary in a way that brings their work to life.

In this way, not only will each learner be encouraged to use particular forms of grammar, punctuation or vocabulary correctly but, essentially, they will gain a strong sense of themselves taking an active role as a writer. It gives them a valuable sense of what it is like to be an author, one who uses grammar not only to improve the quality of their work but also to express themselves as best they can using the written word.

The journey from simply understanding how the English language works to being able to apply that knowledge in order to become a capable and confident writer is a journey that will continue into adulthood and one that, in all truthfulness, never really ends.

However, by providing meaningful activities for both the classroom and beyond, the *Top Class* series can help each and every writer to freely use grammar, punctuation and vocabulary to great effect and support them as they endeavour to bring the written word to life in order to inform, influence and entertain their readers.

*Differentiated activities can be found on the CD Rom.

TOP CLASS - Grammar - Year 3

Plurals

Think about...
Look at the following words:
**foot   wolf   table   baby   tooth
mouse   chair   story   elf   garden**
Put them in the plural form.
Discuss the different ways you can do this.

Guided

You are about to read a story called The Selfish Giant.

Who do you think the giant in this story might be? Draw your answer. Why do you think this giant might be selfish? How might this be shown? How would this make others feel towards the giant? Why might we have presumed the giant to be male and not female?

Once done, answer the questions on page 9.

Independent

You are focusing on how to use and spell a variety of plurals, both regular and irregular.

On your own, with a partner or in a small group; complete the task sheet provided to you by your teacher on page 10.

Once finished, cut off the homework task to take home with you for further practice.

Extension

Imagine you have crept into the Selfish Giant's garden. Complete the task sheet on page 11.

When completed, type up your description and decorate it so that it looks wintry.

Answers

1 Regular: blossoms, birds, trees, furs, chimney-pots, hours, slates
Irregular: children, people

2 There were no daisies and no butterflies in the garden.

3 Snow and Frost were like thieves who had stolen all the flowers and the leaves.

Homework

- No specific answers are required for this task, though teachers should provide opportunities to discuss a variety of mnemonics that will help to remember how to spell these tricky words. Teachers should also refrain from setting this exercise as a test or using it as an assessment opportunity in order that learners are more likely to learn the mnemonic and apply it correctly.

Remember...
We use plurals when there is more than one of something.
This can be done in two ways:
regular: +s, +ies, +ves
irregular: when the singular and plural forms of the noun are spelt differently.

Plurals

The Selfish Giant
Oscar Wilde
Chapter 2

Then the Spring came, and all over the country there were little blossoms and little birds. Only in the garden of the Selfish Giant was it still Winter.

The birds did not care to sing in it as there were no children, and the trees forgot to blossom. Once a beautiful flower put its head out from the grass, but when it saw the notice-board it felt so sorry for the children that it slipped back into the ground again, and went off to sleep.

The only people who were pleased were the Snow and the Frost. 'Spring has forgotten this garden,' they cried, 'so we will live here all the year round.' The Snow covered up the grass with her great white cloak, and the Frost painted all the trees silver. Then they invited the North Wind to stay with them, and he came. He was wrapped in furs, and he roared all day about the garden, and blew the chimney-pots down. 'This is a delightful spot,' he said, 'we must ask the Hail on a visit.' So the Hail came. Every day for three hours he rattled on the roof of the castle till he broke most of the slates, and then he ran round and round the garden as fast as he could go. He was dressed in grey, and his breath was like ice.

'I cannot understand why the Spring is so late in coming,' said the Selfish Giant, as he sat at the window and looked out at his cold white garden; 'I hope there will be a change in the weather.'

But the Spring never came, nor the Summer. The Autumn gave golden fruit to every garden, but to the Giant's garden she gave none. 'He is too selfish,' she said. So it was always Winter there, and the North Wind, and the Hail, and the Frost, and the Snow danced about through the trees.

Look at this Victorian children's classic and answer the questions below.

1 Fill the grid with the nine plurals found in this part of the story. Colour each answer:

Regular (light blue) Irregular (purple)

5 marks

2 Correct this sentence: **There were no daisy and no butterfly in the garden.**
_____

2 marks

3 Correct this sentence: **Snow and Frost were like thief who had stolen all the flower and the leaf.**
_____
_____

3 marks

Plurals

Plurals can be tricky to spell, especially if they are irregular. For each noun listed below, find its plural in the word search. Put each one into a sentence of your own to show that you understand its meaning. When finished, can you spot any rules that might apply to some of the plurals you have used?

Word Search:

R	W	O	M	E	N	F	Q	W	R	E	M
A	I	S	A	S	D	F	N	O	S	L	G
S	S	L	E	A	V	E	S	L	E	P	H
P	H	Z	L	I	M	K	J	V	H	O	J
B	E	S	X	C	R	D	W	E	S	E	C
E	S	E	T	M	U	R	Y	S	U	P	H
R	Q	X	Y	U	K	J	E	N	B	O	I
R	I	O	B	R	A	N	C	H	E	S	L
I	M	F	D	O	A	F	C	J	C	R	D
E	C	H	U	R	C	H	E	S	M	E	R
S	E	O	T	A	T	O	P	T	O	A	E
T	O	M	A	T	O	E	S	P	L	O	N

1. tomato   *tomatoes*
2. cherry
3. raspberry
4. potato
5. leaf
6. bush
7. wolf
8. wish
9. branch
10. fox
11. church
12. man
13. woman
14. child
15. person

Homework

Learn to spell some tricky plurals.
* cherries tomatoes raspberries potatoes
* leaves bushes wolves wishes branches
* foxes churches men women children people

How will you remember each and every one?

Plurals

You have crept into the garden of the Selfish Giant. It is still winter. The Snow and the Frost, the North Wind and the Hail are dancing about through the trees. Describe what you see and hear and, more importantly, what you do not.

Name:

Date:

The Winter Garden

There were no birds chirping and no children laughing. No flowers grew and the trees looked sad and lonely as the frost twinkled like tiny stars from their branches.

Proper Nouns

Think about...
Give an example of the following:
A country and its capital city.
A song and its singer.
A book that is also a film.
Are these common or proper nouns? Why?

Guided

What do you already know about The Wizard of Oz?

Who is its main character? Where does she travel to? How does she get there? Who does she take with her? Why? What happens when she lands in Oz? Who else does she meet while she is there? Who does she have to find and why? Which came first, the book or the film?

Once done, answer the questions on page 13.

Independent

You are considering the difference between common and proper nouns.

On your own, with a partner or in a small group; complete the task sheet provided to you by your teacher on page 14.

Once finished, cut off the homework task to take home with you for further practice.

Extension

Write the start of a story where a storm is approaching. Complete the task on page 15.

Once finished, turn it into an audio book and add sound effects.

Answers

1 Born: New York
Died: Hollywood
The name given to a city is a proper noun.

2 1899: Father Goose, His Book
1900: The Wonderful Wizard of Oz
The title given to a book is a proper noun.

3 Somewhere Over the Rainbow.
The title given to a song is a proper noun.

Homework

- Judy Garland
- Dorothy Gale
- Kansas City, Missouri, USA
- Harold Arlen & Yip Harburg: originally deleted from the film, Roger Edens (Garland's vocal coach) persuaded the producers to put it back in.

Remember...
A noun is a person, place or thing.
A **concrete noun** is physical and can be either:
I. A **common noun** – a person, place or thing.
II. A **proper noun** – the name given to that person, place or thing.

Proper Nouns

Lyman Frank Baum [1856 – 1919]

1856 — Born on May 15th in New York. His father is a barrel maker who goes into the oil business.

1874-1880 — As a teenager he becomes interested in the theatre. His father, now very rich, buys him some theatres to manage.

1881 — Writes a musical: *The Maid of Arran*.

1882 — Marries Maud Gage.

1887-1891 — Father dies. Frank moves to South Dakota with his wife and four sons. Sets up a shop called "Baum's Bazaar". It closes in 1890. Baum starts to run a local newspaper *The Aberdeen Saturday Pioneer*.

1891 — The newspaper fails. Frank and family move to Chicago. He works as a reporter for the *Evening Post*. He also works as a travelling salesman. While away he thinks of stories he can tell his children when he returns home.

1897 — Teams up with illustrator Maxfield Parrish. He publishes his first children's book *Mother Goose in Prose*.

1899 — Teams up with another illustrator William Denslow. He publishes *Father Goose, His Book*. It is the best-selling children's book of the year.

1900 — Baum and Denslow publish another best seller, *The Wonderful Wizard of Oz*. Baum has now written America's best-selling children's book for two years running.

1902 — Baum and Denslow produce *The Wizard of Oz* as a musical. It is a big hit and tours America.

1904 — Begins the second Oz book *The Marvellous Land of Oz*.

1910 — Moves to Hollywood. His home there is known as "Ozcot".

1915-1919 — Falls ill but continues to write more Oz books. He writes one Oz story each year.

1919 — Dies on May 6th.

1920 — His last book *Glinda of Oz* is published.

1939 — The classic film with Judy Garland is released. It wins an Oscar for the song *Somewhere Over the Rainbow*.

Look at this timeline and answer the questions below.

1 List the two American cities in which Lyman F. Baum was born and died.

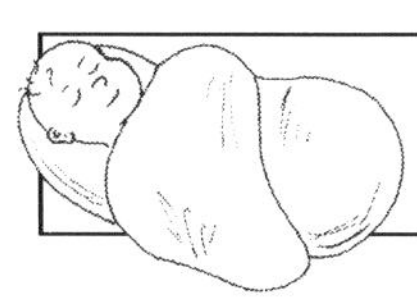

2 marks

What kind of nouns are these? Why?

2 List the two best-selling books Lyman F. Baum wrote between 1899 – 1900.

1899:

1900:

2 marks

What kind of noun are these? Why?

3 Name the song that gained an Oscar in the film The Wizard of Oz in 1939.

1 mark

Proper Nouns

Proper nouns name specific people, places or special things. Since these nouns are names, they always start with a capital letter. When there is more than one part to the name, each part starts with a capital letter. Think of three proper nouns for each box.

Proper Nouns = Names

A Football Team	A Pop Star	A Book	A Clothes Shop

A Theme Park	A Film	A Supermarket	A School

A Pop Band	A Country	A Famous Actor	A TV Programme

Homework

Read about the song Somewhere Over the Rainbow.
- Which actress first sang this song in The Wizard of Oz?
- Which character did this actress play in the same film?
- Where in the film is this song sung?
- Who wrote this song?

Proper Nouns

You are alone on a farm. Suddenly the skies darken and the wind begins to strengthen. You look up and there, in the distance, you spot a twister approaching. Twisting and turning it grows ever closer. Where do you run to when there is no escape?

Name: **Date:**

THE TWISTER

The wheat fields rippled like waves as the wind passed over them and headed towards the farm. Bruce growled and the doors to the cow shed began to clatter and clang. Suddenly, the clothes line broke free and an old shirt flew into the air. There was not a moment to lose.

Pronouns

Think about...
Name the planets in our solar system.
Which are named after Roman gods?
Which is named after a Roman goddess?
What do you know of the Roman god Mars?
Why did the Romans name the 4th planet after him?

Guided

You are looking up some information on Ancient Roman beliefs.

Religion was very important to the Romans but they did not always believe in a single Almighty God. Instead they worshipped twelve main gods and goddesses. Do you know who these were? What did each god or goddess rule over? Which of these gods was the chief? Who was second in command? How popular do you think Mars was with A] soldiers and B] ordinary people? Why do you think this?

Once done, answer the questions on page 17.

Independent

You are considering how to use different kinds of pronouns.

On your own, with a partner or in a small group; complete the task sheet provided to you by your teacher on page 18.

Once finished, cut off the homework task to take home with you for further practice.

Extension

You are the captain of the first spaceship to land on Mars.

Complete the task on page 19.

When finished, type up your log on the computer.

Answers

1 I. religion
II. the lost battle or natural disaster

2 They: The Roman Army
Him: The Roman god Mars

3 Its: it is not two words joined together (it is). It shows possession, in this case the Roman Army is owned by the Roman Empire.

Homework

- Ares – the ancient Greek god of war, its red soil being the colour of blood.
- Surface gravity is 37% less than Earth's meaning you could leap three times higher on Mars.
- Surface temperature: -153°C – 20°C
- 687 days (1.9 Earth years)

Remember...
A **pronoun** is a word that takes the place of a noun.
For example: he, she, it, they, someone, who.

Pronouns

MARS

Religion was an important part of daily life in Ancient Rome. It helped Romans make sense of what was happening in the world. When battles were lost or natural disasters occurred, they believed it was evidence that the gods were unhappy with them. If battles were won or harvests were plentiful, then the Roman people believed they had pleased the gods.

The Romans worshipped a pantheon of gods – a council of twelve major gods. These included six gods: Jupiter, Neptune, Mars, Apollo, Vulcan and Mercury and six goddesses: Juno, Minerva, Venus, Diana, Vesta and Ceres.

In Roman religion, Mars was an incredibly important god. His role was second only to Jupiter, the leader of the gods.

Protector of the Roman Army, Mars himself was the god of war. He was thought to be unpopular with the other gods because he liked to argue and loved conflict. However, Roman soldiers often prayed to Mars for protection before they went into battle, and would ask him to fight on their side.

The Roman Empire was built on the battlefield, its army feared throughout the land.

Although people do not worship the ancient gods today and Romans no longer rule over us, we can still see Mars' name and influence all around us:

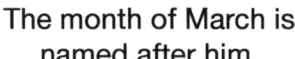
The month of March is named after him.

Mars also gave his name to the Red Planet.

His shield and spear remains the universal symbol for a man.

Look at this information page and answer the questions below.

1 What does the pronoun '**it**' mean in paragraph one?

I. _____

II. _____ *2 marks*

2 What do the pronouns '**they**' and '**his**' refer to in paragraph one?

I. They: _____

II. His: _____ *2 marks*

3 Why does '**its**' not use an apostrophe in paragraph five?

_____
_____ *2 marks*

Pronouns

You are a Reading Detective. Read each sentence. Work out what the word 'it' means. Why do you think writers use pronouns? Do they make the sentence easier or more difficult to read? Why might this be?

What is it?

Dad was angry. The car had broken down and it was raining.			
A. The car	B. Dad's anger	C. The weather	D. Dad
The bird flew to her nest and fed the worm to her chick. It tasted great!			
A. The bird	B. The nest	C. The worm	D. The chick
The painting was ruined. Someone had spilt water on it and the paint had run.			
A. The paint	B. The painting	C. The water	D. Someone
Peter put down his pencil and calculator. The test was hard but at least it was over.			
A. Peter	B. The pencil	C. The test	D. The calculator
Mum looked at her watch. It had stopped. She sighed, picked up her phone and ran to the door.			
A. Mum's watch	B. Mum's sigh	C. Mum's phone	D. The door
We watched Spiderman III yesterday. The film was great! I had a hotdog but it was cold.			
A. The film	B. The cinema	C. The hotdog	D. The weather
Ali closed the book and turned off the light. It was getting late and Ben had school tomorrow.			
A. The book	B. The time	C. School	D. The light
Sanjay looked at the stamp on the envelope. On it was a kangaroo. Inside was a card.			
A. The card	B. The kangaroo	C. The envelope	D. The stamp
It was hopeless. How could Lisa play if her football kit was in the washing machine?			
A. The football kit	B. The football match	C. The situation	D. The washing machine

Homework

Read about the planet Mars.
- Which Greek god is linked to this planet?
- How strong is the gravity on Mars?
- What is the surface temperature on Mars?
- How long does it take Mars to orbit the sun?

Pronouns

You are the captain of the first space mission to step foot on Mars. Write a space diary that describes this historical event. Did the landing go to plan? Did you choose any special words or plant a flag to mark the occasion? How did you feel? How will this achievement help people back home?

| Name: | Date: |

Captain's Log:
For generations, we have looked into the skies and dreamt about setting foot on the Red Planet. Today, that dream has become a reality. Today, we have left footprints on Mars.

Verbs

Think about...
Your teacher will play a game with you.
The game is called Simon Says.
If Simon says it, you must do it.
If he doesn't and you do it, you're out.
Identify the verb in each instruction.

Guided

What other games might you play at a children's party? Make a list with your teacher.

In small groups, choose a game. Write a set of instructions to explain how you play it, keeping them simple so they are easy to understand. Can others recognise which game you have written the instructions for? Identify the verbs in each step of your instructions. Are there any verbs that you could use that would improve your set of instructions? What are they? Why are they useful to know?

Once done, answer the questions on page 21.

Independent

You are looking at how verbs are used when explaining how to play a game.

On your own, with a partner or in a small group; complete the task sheet provided to you by your teacher on page 22.

Once finished, cut off the homework task to take home with you for further practice.

Extension

Create a new party game. Complete the task on page 23.

When finished, invite others to play your new game. Use your set of instructions to help them understand the rules of the game.

Answers

1 Remove, repeat, stands

Note: You may wish to look at the prefix 're' (meaning 'again') in more detail when answering the question so as to allow learners to understand how and why this prefix is often used in instructional text.

2 Dance, swim, hop, find, jump, sit

3 Allow for personal response – discuss word choice and consider what effect this has upon the character walking. Verbs you might like to consider are: limp, tiptoe, creep, race, skip, hobble, stroll.

Homework

- No specific answers are required for this task, though teachers could link this activity with a Data Handling topic during Maths.

Remember...
A **verb** is a word or phrase that describes an action or experience. They are sometimes called 'doing' words.
For example: run, eat, sleep, think, speak and watch are all verbs.

Verbs

Musical Chairs

A party game for young and old alike, this family favourite is easy to set up and fun to play.

Essential Equipment:
Chairs (one less than the number of players)
A CD player and some music.

Instructions:
Step 1: Place the chairs in a row, making sure alternate chairs are facing in the opposite direction.
Step 2: Play the music and get the players to walk around the line of chairs in the same direction.
Step 3: When the music stops, each player must sit on a chair. However, they can only continue in the same direction and can't turn back. The player left standing is out.
Step 4: Remove one of the chairs and repeat steps 1-3 until only the victor stands victorious.

An Alternative Version: Musical Frogs
Instead of placing the chairs in a row, scatter cushions randomly around the room – these will be your lily pads. Leave enough space so that each frog can dance, swim or hop around them while the music plays. When it stops, each frog must find a lily pad to jump onto and sit on. The unlucky amphibian who fails to find the safety of a lily pad is eliminated from the game.

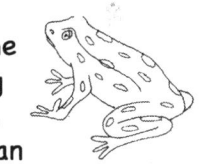

Look at this set of instructions and answer the questions below.

1 List three verbs used in Step 4.

3 marks

2 List six verbs the frog can do while playing Musical Frogs.

3 marks

3 List five ways in which somebody can walk. Act each verb out.

5 marks

Verbs

Look at the list of verbs below. They all mean 'to move'.
Write a sentence that describes how Simon moves.
Draw a picture for each one. Act it out.
What does this verb tell us about Simon?
Is he moving fast or slow, loud or quiet? Why?

Walk with me...

crept	marched	tiptoed	hobbled
bolted			stormed
limped	stumbled	raced	skipped

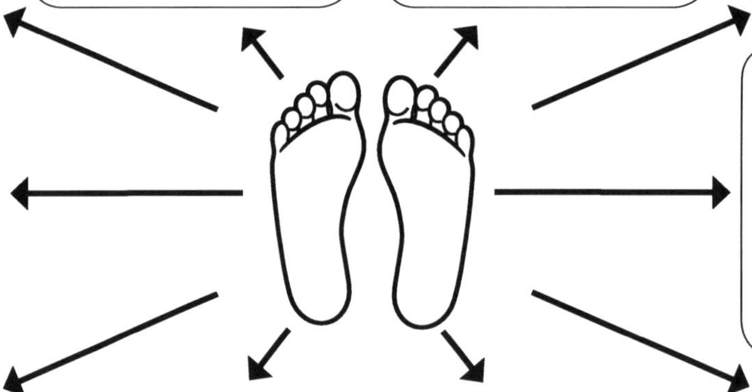

Homework

Design a class survey about their favourite games.
- Which types of games will you ask about?
- How will you collect this information?
- How will you present the results of your survey?
- Did the data you collected surprise you?

Verbs

You have invented a new party game.
What will you call this new game?
How do you play it?
What equipment do you need?
What are its rules?
How do you win?

Name:	Date:

The Game:

Equipment:

How to Play:

Step 1

Step 2

Step 3

Step 4

Step 5

And the winner is...

Modal Verbs

Think about...
Write a sentence that shows:
A] The possibility of you visiting friends tonight. Which modal verb did you use? Why?
B] Whether your best friend is able to swim. Which modal verb did you use? Why?

Guided

You are looking at what makes a good friend. Think about your best friend.

What do you think helps your friendship work? Is it always easy to be a good friend? Why? Why not? What do you do if you fall out with your friend? Why is it worth the effort of being a good friend and trying to restore a friendship after an argument or falling out?

Once done, answer the questions on page 25.

Independent

You are focusing on the use of modal verbs and the effect these have in relation to the possibility of an action taking place.

On your own, with a partner or in a small group; complete the task sheet provided to you by your teacher on page 26.

Once finished, cut off the homework task to take home with you for further practice.

Extension

Write an acrostic poem called Friendship. Complete the task on page 27.

When finished, copy it out and decorate it. Compare your poem with the same poem a friend has written. How is it similar? Is there anything their poem talks about but yours does not?

Answers

1 May: possibility
Would: possibility
Can: ability

2 Might: possibility
May: possibility

Note: You may wish to discuss the shift in formality between these two modal verbs and how, although very similar, they are often used in different situations depending upon who the audience is.

3 Will: ability

Homework

- Randy Newman
- Toy Story (1995)
- Academy Award for Best Original Song & Golden Globe Award for Best Original Song
- No – On both occasions it lost out to Colours of the Wind from Disney's Pocahontas

---

Remember...
A **modal verb** acts differently to ordinary verbs.
The most common modal verbs are: **will, would, should, could, may, can, must** and **might**.
They often describe a possibility or an ability. They can also give advice, instruct or give permission.

Modal Verbs

A Recipe for Friendship

To have many friends in life – to be liked and loved by all those around you, you will need:

- ♥ ***A generous spirit*** – You may well think this means buying gifts. You would be wrong! Even though it is great to give a thoughtful present from time to time, two of the most important things you can give someone are your time and a listening ear. Don't be a 'me monster'.
- ♥ ***Some kind words*** – Don't be embarrassed to tell them what you like about them. Be positive and use words that will build up your friendship rather than tear it down. Help them to feel good about themselves. Remember, you are trying to build a new friendship, not destroy one. A hurtful word can cause damage to a friendship, making it difficult to repair.
- ♥ ***A helping hand*** – When you see somebody struggling with their homework or perhaps standing alone in the playground, why not go over to them? Give them the answers (but only when your teacher isn't in sight) or ask them to participate in whatever game you are playing. Don't keep friends to yourself. Share them! Nobody likes selfish people. The world is big enough for everyone to enjoy themselves.
- ♥ ***A pinch of courage*** – Don't be put off trying to start a new friendship with somebody you haven't spoken to before. You might have lots in common. Who knows, they may turn out to be your future best friend.
- ♥ ***A sprinkle of laughter*** – Nobody wants to be in the company of someone that never makes them laugh. Don't be too serious. Enjoy yourself, and like butterflies to a summer garden, friends will always be attracted to you.

Simply mix all the ingredients together and store in a warm heart. When you are ready to serve, add love and dish out immediately. Stand back and watch as new friendships are created or old ones are made stronger.

Look at this advice and answer the questions below.

1 List the three modal verbs in 'A generous spirit'. Do they show ability or possibility?

I. _____

II. _____

III. _____

3 marks

2 List the two modal verbs in 'A pinch of courage'. Do they show ability or possibility?

I. _____

II. _____

2 marks

3 Which modal verb is used in the by-line? Does it show ability or possibility?

_____

1 mark

Modal Verbs

You are looking at positive and negative modal verbs. Match each positive modal verb to their negative. Use a different colour for each pair. Once done, complete the quiz below. Check your answers with a friend. Together, think of two more quiz questions to ask another pair.

Quiz Questions

Positive	Sentence	Negative
can	I've not seen her in a long time. I _____ recognise her now. (*wouldn't, shouldn't*)	wouldn't
will	We're lost! We _____ turned left. (*could have, should have*)	couldn't
should	You _____ be hungry. You've just had your dinner. (*can, can't*)	mustn't
	Mum's purse is not here. She _____ gone shopping. (*mustn't have, must have*)	
could	I _____ be able to play for weeks. I've broken my leg. (*won't, shouldn't*)	can't
must	I _____ take an umbrella. It looks like it will rain later. (*would, wouldn't*)	won't
	Dad says he _____ pick us up after the film but mum will instead. (*can, can't*)	
would	I _____ go to the party. I was working. (*could, couldn't*)	shouldn't

---

Homework

Read about the song *You've Got a Friend in Me*.
- Who wrote this song?
- In which film did it first appear?
- Name two awards that it was nominated for.
- Did it win either of these two awards?

Modal Verbs

You are a poet. Think about what makes a good friend. How do you show somebody you care about them by what you say and how you act?
Write an acrostic poem that helps put these ideas down into a piece of poetic verse.

Name:	Date:

F ....

R ....

I ....

E ....

N ....

D ....

S ....

H ....

I ....

P ....

Adverbs

Think about...
Look at these words:
quickly quietly eagerly slowly nervously boldly bravely
What makes them adverbs?
How and why might each be used?

Guided

You are considering how and why an author might use an adverb.

Using the words listed above, complete the following sentence and discuss what implication (negative or positive) each one has on the meaning of the sentence itself:

Sam stepped _____ onto Skeleton Island.

Once done, answer the questions on page 29.

Independent

You are focusing on why an author might use an adverb and how this can alter the meaning of a sentence.

On your own, with a partner or in a small group; complete the task sheet provided to you by your teacher on page 30.

Once finished, cut off the homework task to take home with you for further practice.

Extension

Imagine you are one of the crew who volunteered to go to Skeleton Island. Complete the task on page 31.

When completed, type up your adventure and compare it with another crew member's story.

Answers

1 Gently – they would not want to rush or be heavy handed with the lifeboat for fear of tipping the volunteers into the sea or damaging the boat itself. This adverb shows they were being careful.

2 Dangerously low – although they had some provisions left, it was not enough to sustain the crew for very much longer. This adverb shows the need to go to the island.

3 Allow for personal response – again use the adverbs listed above and explore their impact upon both the sentence and the reader.

Homework

- No specific answers are required for this task, though teachers should check how authentic each map of Skeleton Island is.

Remember...
An **adverb** modifies the meaning of a verb. It gives us more information about how, when, where or why an action is taking place. Usually an adverb will end +ly but this is not always the case.

Adverbs

THE FOG

The nearer Skeleton Island we sailed, the thicker and heavier the fog would become.

As we caught a glimpse of the island, a cold grey blanket of cloud wrapped itself around us and held us firmly in its grip. We were its prisoner, the captain not daring to sail further for fear of colliding with the rocky shore.

After three days of waiting for the fog to lift, and with food and water getting dangerously low (even fish seemed to have fled the murky depths) it was decided to send a small party of the crew ashore.

One of the lifeboats was lowered gently into the water, myself and five others having volunteered to step aboard. If I knew then of the horrors that awaited us, then I would not have placed a single toe inside that boat nor lifted a single finger to help row.

Sometimes walls are built to stop people getting in.
  Sometimes walls are built to stop things getting out.
   Only now do I realise that the fog was there not to do us harm but to protect us. If only we had listened… then Jacobs and Peterson would still be with us and I would not be sat here alone wondering if I would ever see my captain and my shipmates ever again.

Look at this diary extract and answer the questions below.

1 How was the lifeboat lowered into the water? Why might this be?

I. How: _____

II. Why: _____

2 marks

2 How and why does the writer describe how much food and water is aboard the ship?

I. How: _____

II. Why: _____

2 marks

3 How and why might the crew have stepped onto Skeleton Island?

I. How: _____

II. Why: _____

2 marks

Adverbs

You are reading the diary of each crew member that stepped onto Skeleton Island. How do they describe their first steps? Underline the adverb in each extract. What does it tell us about their character? How are they feeling?

Dear Diary:

Diary	Adverb	What does this tell us?
Foolishly, I stepped onto the island.	foolishly	He thinks it was a mistake going to Skeleton Island.
Slowly, I stepped onto the island.		
Eventually, I stepped onto the island.		
I stepped quietly onto the island.		
I stepped shakily onto the island.		
Quickly, I stepped onto the island.		
Gingerly, I stepped onto the island.		
I stepped boldly onto the island.		

Homework

Create a map of Skeleton Island.
- What will you find on this island?
- Which places might you visit?
- Which places might you want to avoid?
- How will you make your map look old and real?

Adverbs

You are lost and alone on Skeleton Island. All you have is a pencil and a single piece of paper. Write to your crew telling them how this came to be. Do you cling to the hope that your message will never need to be read or do you fear that your message will only be discovered alongside your dry and dusty bones?

| Name: | Date: |

How long I have been on this island, I cannot say. Nor do I know if I will ever escape and return to my ship. But my story must be told.

I hope that you never read this tale and that one day, I will tell you of my great adventure and eventual escape myself. In case I am unable to do so, I put my final words down on this paper and ask you to pray for my soul.

Adjectives

Think about...
Why do people use guard dogs?
What breeds are usually used? Why?
Ancient Greeks believed a dog guarded Hades.
What might it look like? Draw a sketch. Add notes.
Compare your ideas with the monster Cerberus.

Guided	Answers
You are looking at the ancient Greek dog Cerberus. What is strange about this dog? How scary does it look? Why? Where does it live? What job does it do? Who were Cerberus' parents? When would the ancient Greeks believe they might see Cerberus? Why do you think they believed in such a vicious and scary creature? Once done, answer the questions on page 33.	**1** I. inky black eyes II. razor sharp teeth III. shiny black coat IV. sweeping dragon's tail **2** Deep dark shadows **3** In <u>Greek</u> mythology, Typhon was a <u>huge</u> <u>fire-breathing</u> dragon with <u>glowing</u> <u>red</u> eyes. *Note: Spend time exploring the meaning of each of these adjectives: what do they tell us about each monster and why might the author have chosen to use them?*
Independent You are focusing on how to categorise a variety of adjectives and use them with increased proficiency to improve your writing. On your own, with a partner or in a small group; complete the task sheet provided to you by your teacher on page 34. Once finished, cut off the homework task to take home with you for further practice.	
Extension	**Homework**
You are creating a mythical beast of your very own. Complete the task on page 35. When finished, give your description to a classmate and ask them to draw your monstrous creature. Compare it to the one that you have drawn to illustrate your piece of writing.	• No specific answers are required for this task, though teachers should ensure that models include a brief description that includes the use of adjectives.

Remember...
When describing a noun using more than one **adjective**, it is important that we place the describing words in the correct order before the noun. This is as follows: first size, then shape, followed by age, colour, origin, material, opinion, observation and purpose.

Adjectives

Cerberus

In ancient Greek mythology, there is a gigantic three-headed dog who guards the entrance to the Underworld, a place where the spirits of the dead can enter but none are permitted to leave.

Feared by the spirits, this vicious creature will devour anyone who dares try to escape.

Its father is Typhon – the mightiest and deadliest monster in Greek mythology. A huge fire-breathing dragon said to have glowing red eyes, a hundred heads and a hundred wings. Even the Olympian gods are petrified of this beast.

Its mother is Echidna – a half-woman, half-snake creature known as 'the mother of all monsters.' With her beautiful face, she lures passers-by into her cave and then eats them raw in the deep dark shadows.

No wonder Cerberus looks so terrifying!

The Hound of Hades

- A shiny black coat the colour of death.
- Three snarling heads: one past, one present, one future.
- Inky black eyes that turn you to stone if peered into.
- Razor sharp teeth and a poisonous bite.
- Saliva that turns into deadly Wolf's Bane when dripped on the ground.
- Mighty lion's paws and claws.

Look at this web page and answer the questions below.

1 Which adjectives are used to describe the different parts of Cerberus?

Eyes: _____ Teeth: _____

Coat: _____ Tail: _____

4 marks

2 Which two adjectives are used to describe the shadows of Echidna's cave?

1 mark

3 Underline the adjectives in the following sentence.

In Greek mythology, Typhon was a huge fire-breathing dragon with glowing red eyes.

5 marks

TOP CLASS - Grammar - Year 3

Adjectives

You are an ancient Greek. Research which mythical beasts are pictured below. Choose one to describe. What does it look like? Where does it live? What does it guard? Why is it feared? What are its strengths? How can it be defeated?

Mythical Monsters

- The Minotaur
- Medusa
- The Cyclops
- The Griffin
- The Hydra
- Pegasus

Homework

Create a model of an ancient Greek monster. Like any piece of art, include a brief description that you can place next to your model when it goes on display.

Adjectives

You are an ancient Greek.
Create a monster that the gods of Olympus will fear.
What does it look like? Where does it live?
Why is it feared so greatly? What does it guard?
What are its strengths? How can it be defeated?

Name:

Date:

What does it look like?

Where does it live?

What does it guard?

How did it come to be?

Why is it feared so greatly?

How can it be defeated?

What are its strengths?

TOP CLASS - Grammar - Year 3

Conjunctions

Think about...
Look at these two sentences:
We can either fight the alien or flee.
We can neither fight the alien nor flee.
Which word is the conjunction in each?
How else are the two sentences different?

Guided

Look at the following acronym: FANBOYS.

These letters help us to remember special words known as co-ordinating conjunctions. These are: for, and, nor, but, or, yet, so. Can you think of a sentence that uses one of these words? Write it on a wipe board and underline the co-ordinating conjunction. Share your sentence with your teacher and discuss how the conjunction affects the meaning of the sentence as a whole.

Once done, answer the questions on page 37.

Independent

You are considering how and when to use a variety of co-ordinating conjunctions.

On your own, with a partner or in a small group; complete the task sheet provided to you by your teacher on page 38.

Once finished, cut off the homework task to take home with you for further practice.

Extension

You have sixty seconds to defeat the alien and escape. Complete the task on page 39.

When finished, compare your ending with a partner's. Discuss which ending you think readers would enjoy the most and why this might be.

Answers

1
I. To join two words together: dark and deadly

II. To join two phrases together: as dark and as deadly as

III. To join two sentences together: [A] Its long, thin tail whipped the air. Acid dripped from its gaping mouth.
[B] Crimson eyes stared straight ahead. Teller knew that it was about to attack.

2 To highlight the two opposing options that Teller had to choose between.

3 Yet – allow for personal response that draws attention to the humour of this sentence.

Homework

- Extra-Terrestrial
- May 26th, 1882 (Cannes)
  June 11th, 1982 (USA)
- Steven Spielberg
- 114 minutes (1 hour 24 mins)

Remember...
A conjunction is a word that links two words
or sentences together. Think of them as gluing words.
Coordinating conjunctions are sometimes also referred
to with the acronym **FANBOYS**:
for, and, nor, but, or, yet, so.

Conjunctions

Intruder Alert

The alien was coal-black. Its fangs were dark and deadly, as dark and as deadly as its talons. Its long, thin tail whipped the air and acid dripped from its gaping mouth. Crimson eyes stared straight ahead and Teller knew that it was about to attack.

Self-destruct in three minutes and counting.

But what choice did he have: blow up the ship and kill the beast or save the ship and risk carrying it back to Jupiter Station?

He had made up his mind – a ship could be rebuilt from scratch. People, on the other hand, could not.

Self-destruct in two minutes and counting.

The ship was eerily silent. The handful of crew that had survived were now safely off the ship. There was one last escape pod left and it had Teller's name on it.

There was just a small matter of having to get past a coal-black, man-eating alien; yet something told him that asking it politely to move to one side was not going to help.

Time was running out. In fact, time was not just running out, it was sprinting.

Self-destruct in one minute and counting.

Teller had to think fast… No, not fast. Fast was too slow. Teller had to think incredibly fast. There wasn't a second to lose. Well, if we are being very precise, there were exactly sixty seconds to lose but who's counting!

Look at this cliff hanger and answer the questions below.

1 How is the conjunction **'and'** used in three different ways in paragraph one?

I. _____

II. _____

III. _____

3 marks

2 Why has the writer used the conjunction **'or'** in paragraph three?

_____

_____

2 marks

3 Which conjunction is used in paragraph seven? How is this conjunction used?

_____

_____

2 marks

Conjunctions

You are playing Conjunction Connect Four.
Cut out and make the dice below.
Once made, play the game with a partner.
A larger version of the dice and grid is available on the CD Rom.

Connect Four

A game for two players.

You will need: A conjunction dice and some counters of two different colours.

How to play: Each player takes it in turn to roll the dice. When the dice stops it will give you two conjunctions to choose from. Put one of them into a sentence. If it makes sense, collect a counter and place it on the board. If it does not make sense, the other player can make a challenge. When a conjunction is used wrongly, no counter is collected. Once a conjunction has been used by a player, that player cannot use it again. The winner is the first player to make a line of four counters of the same colour.

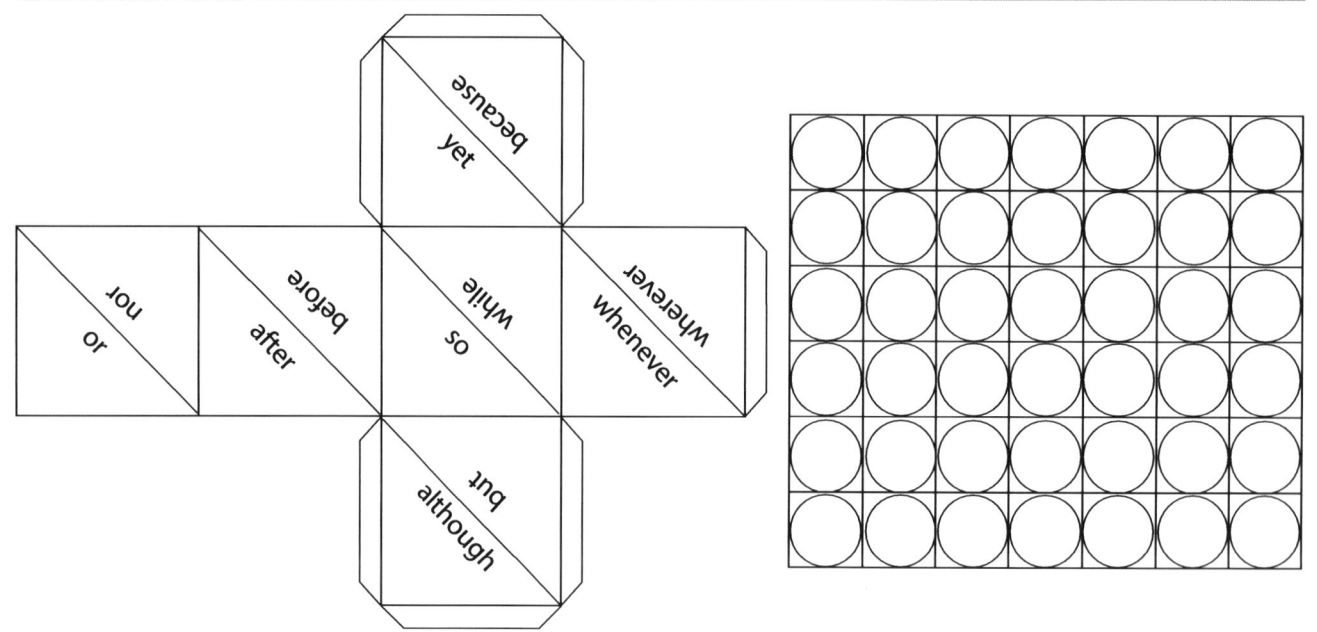

Homework

Read about the film E.T.
- What do the letters E.T. stand for?
- When was this children's film first released?
- Who directed this film?
- How long is the film?

Conjunctions

You have sixty seconds before your spaceship explodes. Sixty seconds to make it to the last escape pod. There is just one small problem… a deadly alien stands in your way. It's not a huge problem, just one that you need to solve pretty fast if you want to get off the ship alive!

Name:	Date:

There was one last escape pod left and it had my name on it.

There was just a small matter of having to get past a coal-black, man-eating alien; yet something told me that asking it politely to move to one side was not going to help.

Time was running out. In fact, time was not just running out, it was sprinting.

Self-destruct in one minute and counting.

I had to think fast… No, not fast. Fast was too slow. I had to think incredibly fast. There wasn't a second to lose. Well, if we are being very precise, there were exactly sixty seconds to lose but who's counting!

Present Continuous

Think about...
Look at these words:
tornado   twister   cyclone
What are they?
Watch a film clip of a tornado or twister.
How strong and dangerous are they?

Guided

You are about to read a shape poem called Tornado.

Do you think this poem will be written in straight lines? Why? Why not? What shape do you think it will take? Why? Do you think the writer might also play with how the words are placed in the poem? Why might the writer do this? When reading the poem aloud, how might it be read? Why?

Note: This poem has been taken from Reading Explorers Year 3 and the accompanying audio is available in Reading Explorers Aloud! Year 3 (Track 22).

Once done, answer the questions on page 41.

Independent

You are considering the spelling rules we need to apply when using the continuous form.

On your own, with a partner or in a small group; complete the task sheet provided to you by your teacher on page 42.

Once finished, cut off the homework task to take home with you for further practice.

Extension

You are presenting a live news report. Complete the task on page 43.

When you have finished, recreate the broadcast using green screen and a strong fan.

Answers

1 swirling, twisting, swishing, trembling

2 Allow for personal response but one that draws attention to letters being moved to echo the movement of the tornado, the growing in size of the words as the tornado grows in strength and the trembling font being used for the knocking of knees to show they are scared.

3 is raining, is pouring, is snoring.

Note: You may wish to look at the spelling rule for +ing with regards to verbs that end with an e (snore).

Homework

- No specific answers are required for this task, though learners should be able to explain why they have placed a word under a particular rule.

Remember...
We use the **present continuous** to describe an on-going action that is happening now. It can also describe a mood. For example: We are not walking to school today because it's raining. Mum is driving us there instead. How exciting!

Present Continuous

Look at this shape poem and answer the questions below.

1 List the four verbs that use the present continuous.

2 marks

2 Why do you think the poet has written these words strangely?

_____

_____

3 marks

3 Underline the present continuous in this nursery rhyme.

It's raining; it's pouring. The old man is snoring.

He went to bed and bumped his head. So, couldn't get up in the morning.

3 marks

Present Continuous

Spelling words that end +ing can be tricky. Cut out the rule grid below. Make sure you only cut along the dotted lines so all four flaps open. Glue the spine of the grid into your book. Use the rules to group the +ing words together under each correct flap.

+ ing:

Rule 1:		Rule 2:
Short vowel sound followed by two consonants = Just +ing	joke, run, talk, bake, drink, put, jump, paint, swim, lift, nod, make / play, rain, sing, write, turn, know, stand, drive, shop, eat, chat, have	Short vowel sound followed by one consonant = Double the consonant then +ing
Rule 3:		**Rule 4:**
Ending in 'e' = Drop the 'e' then +ing		Long vowel sound = Just +ing

Homework

Go on an +ing hunt. Find five examples for each of the four spelling rules from a book you are reading in class or at home. Choose one word from each rule and put it in a sentence of your own.

Present Continuous

You are a TV news reporter. A disaster has hit your local area and you are sent to report on what has happened. Who do you interview? What do you ask them? How do they reply?

Name: **Date:**

Channel 7 News

News Reader: We can go straight to our reporter now, live on Haystack Hill. Tell us, what is happening over there?

Reporter: Thanks Bruce. Well, as you can see, it looks as if a tornado has swept right through this area and brushed everything to one side. Just look at this mess! But here with me now is Mr Pig of Yellow Grass Grove. Mr Pig, can you tell us what happened?

Mr Pig:

Reporter:

Mr Pig:

Reporter:

Mr Pig:

Reporter:

Mr Pig:

Reporter: Well, that's all for now. This is _____, reporting live on Haystack Hill for Channel Seven News. Now back to the studio.

News Reader: Thanks _____, and we will have more on that breaking news as and when it happens.

TOP CLASS - Grammar - Year 3

Past Continuous

Think about...
What are ants known for?
Why do ants store food in the summer?
Do you think this is a good idea? Why?
Why might others disagree with the ant and say...
"All work and no play makes Jack a dull boy."

Guided

You are looking at an Aesop fable called The Ant and the Grasshopper.

If the ant is seen as hard working, what type of character do you think the grasshopper will be? Why? If Mr Grasshopper wants to play but Mrs Ant wants to work, what do you predict might happen in this fable. Why? If your prediction is correct, what might the moral of this fable be?

Once done, answer the questions on page 45.

Independent

You are focusing on how and when to use the singular (was) and plural (were) form of the past continuous.

On your own, with a partner or in a small group; complete the task sheet provided to you by your teacher on page 46.

Once finished, cut off the homework task to take home with you for further practice.

Extension

Which personality are you more like: an ant or a grasshopper? Complete the task on page 47.

Consider why it is important to have a balanced view of work and play. If you haven't, what might you change so that you are able to enjoy life to the full.

Answers

1 Mr Grasshopper: was hopping, was chirping, was singing
Mrs Ant: was carrying

2 Mr Grasshopper: (was not) wasn't hopping, wasn't chirping, wasn't singing

3 Allow for personal response.
I. were flying
II. was sailing
III. were playing
IV. was sitting

Homework

- No specific answers are required for this task, though learners should have used the correct spelling of the continuous form together with the correct grammatical use of *was* and *were*.

Note: An A4 colour version of the image supplied on page 46 is available on the CD Rom.

Remember...
We use the **past continuous** to describe an on-going action that happened in the past. We use **was** for the singular and **were** for the plural. For example: Peter was running. The children were playing.

Past Continuous

The Ant & the Grasshopper

It was summer and Mr Grasshopper was hopping about, chirping and singing to his heart's content. Mrs Ant passed by, carrying food on her back, back to her nest.
"Why don't you come dance with me," asked Mr Grasshopper, "instead of toiling your life away?"
"I am helping store up food for winter," replied Mrs Ant, "and I recommend you do the same."
"Why bother about winter?" laughed Mr Grasshopper. "We have plenty of food at present."
Mrs Ant shook her head, bid him good day and continued to make her way back home.
Winter came and Mr Grasshopper found himself dying of hunger.
He no longer hopped. He no longer chirped. He no longer sang.
Instead, he watched the ants handing out corn that they had collected during happier times.
MORAL: Working hard today will benefit you tomorrow.

The Ant Personality: They plan for the future and want to enjoy the fruits of their labour. They are quite strict about when they work. As a result, they are more likely to be successful in the long run but may seem to have a dull and boring life.

The Grasshopper Personality: They are carefree and relaxed about work. They believe you should enjoy life today and be happy. As a result, they are more likely to be seen as having an exciting life but may struggle when life becomes difficult in the future.

The Key to Happiness: strike a balance between work and play. Just think what life would have been like for both characters if Mrs Ant had danced in the summer and Mr Grasshopper had helped her carry an ear of corn back home.

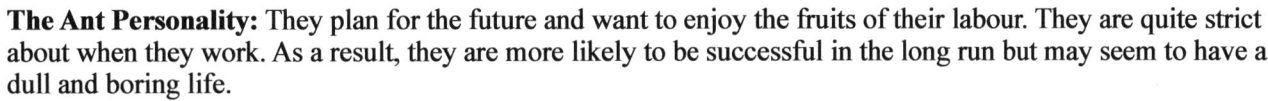

Look at this PSHE text and answer the questions below.

1 What were Mr Grasshopper and Mrs Ant doing at the start of the fable? Lines 1-2.

Mr Grasshopper: _____

Mrs Ant: _____ *4 marks*

2 What was Mr Grasshopper not doing at the end of the fable? Line 8.

Mr Grasshopper: _____ *3 marks*

3 Use **was** and **were** to complete the following sentences:

I. The birds _____ high above the sea.

II. The boat _____ across the ocean.

III. The boys and girls _____ in the playground.

IV. Their teacher _____ on the bench. *4 marks*

TOP CLASS - Grammar - Year 3

Past Continuous

Yesterday you visited the park. You want to tell a friend what was happening while you were there. Look at the picture below and describe the events that you experienced. What did you see? What did you hear?

What Happened Yesterday?

was	were
The dog was barking at the cat.	The twins were crying in the pram.

Homework

Write a short diary extract that tells the reader about what you did during the last school holidays. What did you do? Did you do it alone or with friends or family? Was it fun and exciting, surprising or interesting?

Past Continuous

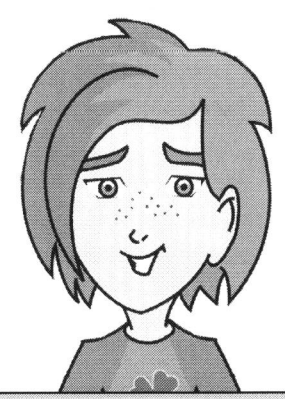

Some people are like Mrs Ant, working hard today so they can live well in the future. Others are like Mr Grasshopper, enjoying today and not worrying about the future. Why might different people have different points of view? Conclude by writing about what you believe and explain why you think this.

Name:	Date:

I'd rather be an ant personality | **I'd rather be a grasshopper personality**

The Infinitive

Think about...
Why do people grow their own food?
Why not just buy it from a supermarket?
Have you ever grown or picked your own food?
Yes: What did you grow or pick and from where?
No: Would you like to? Why? Why not?

Guided

You are reading a gardening book on how to start growing your own food.

Do you think the instructions will be short and simple or long and complicated? Why might this be?

Once done, answer the questions on page 49.

Independent

You are considering how and when to use the infinitive in instructional writing.

On your own, with a partner or in a small group; complete the task sheet provided to you by your teacher on page 50.

Once finished, cut off the homework task to take home with you for further practice.

Extension

You are a keen gardener. Complete the task on page 51.

When finished, consider how you might grow fruit or veg at school and why this is important.

Answers

1 to grow, to harvest, to eat.
They have been written in their natural chronological order.

2 to use, to snap, to pinch
twist, stop, remember

3 Audience: the beginner gardener.
Purpose: allow for personal response but one that explores and explains some of the following possible ideas that go beyond 'to instruct' and touches upon to educate, to encourage and to inspire.

Homework

- No specific answers are required for this task, though teachers could link this practical activity to topics in Maths or Science.

Remember...
The infinitive is the basic form of a verb. They are often used in instructions because they tell you what to do. However, the infinitive can also come after the word 'to' when describing a general action or when describing its purpose.

48   **TOP CLASS** - Grammar - Year 3

The Infinitive

Grow Your Own Green Beans

Easy to grow, easy to harvest, easy to eat. Green beans are a great starter crop for the beginner gardener.

Before rushing out to buy your packet of beans, you must first decide which variety of plant you would like to grow: pole beans – climbing vines that will need supporting or bush beans – short, compact plants that need no support.

How to grow your green beans:
As a rule of thumb, beans need to be planted in warm soil, well after the danger of frost returning. They prefer to grow in rich fertile soil so digging in some organic compost will help give your plants the best start in life.

Each seed will need to be planted about an inch (2.5 cm) deep and watered to stay evenly moist until all of the seedlings have emerged from the ground. If the soil dries out, your seeds are unlikely to germinate.

Once your seedlings have several leaves, cover the garden beds with mulch to keep the soil damper and cooler in the hot summer months. This will also help prevent weeds from growing.

Your crop should be ready for picking around sixty days after planting.

Don't be tempted to leave them to grow too long as older beans become stringy and are tough to eat; smaller beans are sweeter and more tender so picking them regularly is ideal.

When picking, it is always a good idea to use both hands to snap or twist them from the stem or to use the one-handed approach which uses the thumb and finger to pinch the stem of the bean. This will help stop you ripping, tearing and damaging the plant. Remember, a healthy happy plant will give you more beans!

Look at this gardening article and answer the questions below.

1 Look at line one. List the three infinitives and explain why they are written in this order.

_____ *2 marks*

2 Read the conclusion. Fill in the table below.

The infinitive			The infinitive		
to	to	to			

6 marks

3 Who do you think this text has been written for and why?

Audience: _____

Purpose: _____ *2 marks*

TOP CLASS - Grammar - Year 3

The Infinitive

You want to grow some cress. Why might this be a good idea, especially if you don't have a garden? How easy do you think it will be? What could you eat your cress with? Complete the instructions using the infinitive labels below. Follow the instructions to make your own Cress Head!

How to Make a Cress Head!

You will need: A hard-boiled egg & an egg cup, a packet of cress seeds, a piece of paper towel, some cotton wool, a butter knife, a teaspoon and some felt tip pens _____ your egg.

1. Ask an adult _____ you _____ an egg.
2. When cold enough _____ , use the back of the butter knife _____ open the top.
3. Use your spoon _____ the egg and carefully wash the empty shell.
4. Wet a small piece of paper towel and place it inside the empty shell. Put the cotton wool on top _____ the water from evaporating.
5. Scatter a layer of cress seeds on the cotton wool. Sprinkle on some water for the cress _____ .
6. Decorate your egg with a funny face _____ it unique and easy _____ . Remember not _____ any hair on your design.
7. Leave in a warm, light place, remembering _____ with drops of water every day.
8. The seeds should begin _____ in two days and your egg will begin _____ like it is growing hair!
9. When the hair is 5cm long (in about a week) visit the barbers _____ it a haircut!
10. If you want _____ more, simply replace the old cotton wool and paper towel and start again.

To sprinkle	To make	To grow	To drink
To help	To stop	To handle	To give
To sprout	To boil	To draw	To remove
To identify	To decorate	To crack	To look

Homework

Enter a class sunflower growing competition. Start growing your sunflower seeds at school. When you take the seedlings home, remember to water and feed them. The winner of the competition will be the person who can grow the tallest sunflower by the end of the year.

The Infinitive

You are a budding gardener. Write a letter to your Head Teacher to persuade them to include gardening in the curriculum. What would you grow? How will it help your school and your learning? How will it help your health and well-being?

Name:	Date:

Use the checklist below to help you write your letter.

A Letter to Persuade

☐ I start my letter with 'Dear'.

☐ I then write their full name and title.

☐ I put a comma after their name.

☐ I tell them why I am writing.

☐ I give reasons why having a garden in school is a good thing. This includes:

  ☐ What we will learn about plants and other wildlife.

  ☐ How it will help us learn about healthy eating and caring for the environment.

  ☐ How nature helps people to relax and be happy.

  ☐ What other lessons we will learn about being patient and how to work with others.

☐ My last paragraph asks the Head Teacher to think carefully about why gardens are important.

☐ I suggest where the garden might be put.

☐ I end my letter with a formal phrase.

☐ I sign off my letter with my full name and sign it.

Past Simple I

Think about...
Look at these verbs:
**live   walk   dance   help   play
eat   skip   chat   try   read**
Put them in the simple past.
How are the similar? How do they differ?

Guided

You are about to read a fable called The Lion and the Mouse.

What is a fable? How old are they? What makes them so special? Why were fables often spoken rather than written down? Would you rather listen to a fable being read or read it yourself? Why? In which of these two ways do you think you are most likely to understand the fable, learn its moral and act upon it? Why do you think this? Share your ideas with your teacher.

Once done, answer the questions on page 53.

Independent

You are considering how to spell words when they are written in the simple past, both regular and irregular.

On your own, with a partner or in a small group; complete the task sheet provided to you by your teacher on page 54.

Once finished, cut off the homework task to take home with you for further practice.

Extension

You are thinking about the art of storytelling. Complete the task on page 55.

Once finished, choose a fable and practise being a storyteller to an audience of your peers.

Answers

1 awakened, placed, yawned, opened.
Rule: +ed at the end of the verb.

Note: focus on why 'placed' differs from the other verbs

2 cried, scurried, replied.
Rule: replace the y with an i +ed.

3 Paragraph one: was, slept
Paragraph five: forgot
Paragraph six: was, caught, knew

Homework

- In the wild: 12-16 years
  In captivity: up to 25 years
- A lion needs 7kg or more per day
  A lioness needs around 5kg per day
- Lions usually hunt from dusk till dawn. Female lions do 85-90% of the hunting, whilst the male lions patrol the territory and protect the pride.
- 114 decibels – that's about 25 times louder than a lawn mower.

Remember...
The **simple past** tells us that something happened in the past and is now over. This is done by changing the spelling of the verb in two ways: **regular**: +ed, +d, +ied or **irregular**: when the verb in the past tense is spelt differently and doesn't end in any of the three regular forms above.

Past Simple I

The Lion and the Mouse

Once there was a lion sleeping in the shade, dreaming of hunting for prey. While he slept, a tiny mouse brushed past him on his way home.

This awakened the lion, who placed his huge paw upon him. 'I could do with a light snack,' he yawned and opened his big jaws to swallow him up.

'Pardon me, O King,' cried the little mouse. 'Forgive me for disturbing you. It was but an accident and I have heard of your wisdom as well as your strength. If you do let me go, then I will be in your gratitude forever and will one day return this favour.'

The Lion was so tickled at the idea of the tiny mouse being able to help him, that he lifted his paw and chuckled as he scurried away.

Seasons passed and the Lion forgot all about his funny little friend and his little act of kindness.

One day, the elderly lion was caught in a hunter's trap. Try as he might, the lion could not escape the heavy rope that was tied around his neck and he knew that his days were numbered.

Just then, the tiny mouse happened to pass by. Upon seeing the lion's sadness, he climbed up his mane and began gnawing away at the ropes that bound him.

'It's no use, little friend. The hunters will soon be here.' But the tiny mouse said nothing and continued to gnaw at the rope until he had chewed right through it.

The King of the Beasts was free!
'Now I remember you,' said the grateful lion.
'As I remember you,' replied the mouse.

Look at this Aesop fable and answer the questions below.

1 Read paragraph two. List four examples of the simple past. Explain their spelling rule.

☐ ☐ ☐ ☐   ☐

2 marks

2 Find the simple past of the following verbs in the text. Explain their spelling rule.

cry: scurry: reply:

_____   ☐

4 marks

3 List the examples of the irregular simple past in the following paragraphs:

Paragraph one: _____

Paragraph five: _____

Paragraph six: _____   ☐

3 marks

Past Simple I

Cut out the words below. Shuffle them and place them face down. Take turns with a partner to choose two cards. If the two verbs match, keep them. Each pair must then identify the simple past word and put it into a sentence. The winner will have the most cards when there are no more cards to turn over.

The Past is Simple!

go	took	wrote	speak	drive
flew	caught	slept	write	bought
drink	buy	make	catch	take
made	break	fly	do	broke
ran	did	went	ate	run
eat	spoke	drove	drank	sleep

Homework

Learn about the King of the Jungle.
- For how long do lions live?
- How much meat do lions need to eat daily?
- Who does most of the hunting: lions or lionesses?
- How loud is a lion's roar?

Past Simple I

You are going to read a fable to younger children. Which fable will you pick? What will you need to think about when choosing your fable? How will you read it? Will you ask any questions about what you have read? What questions might these be? What lesson do you hope they will learn?

Name:	Date:

The fable I would like to read is...	
I picked this fable because...	When I practise my reading, I think I am good at...
The lesson this fable teaches is...	How will I start my fable?

	When I practise my reading, I think I need to remember...

When reading, how will I make sure that I am a good storyteller?

The questions I would like to ask about the fable are...

★	★
★	★

TOP CLASS - Grammar - Year 3

55

Past Simple II

Think about...
What happened to the Titanic?
Where and when did it sink?
Why did it sink?
Why is the sinking of this ship so famous?
What do you already know about its passengers?

Guided

You are about to read the actual words from eight year old Marshall Drew who was aboard the Titanic when it sank that fateful night.

What do you think he will say? What will we learn from him that we don't already know? Why do you think he survived the disaster when many others did not? Do you think it is important for historians to read eye witness accounts? Why? Why might historians have to be careful when reading such accounts?

Once done, answer the questions on page 57.

Independent

You are reconsidering how to spell words when they are written in the simple past, both regular and irregular.

On your own, with a partner or in a small group; complete the task sheet provided to you by your teacher on page 58.

Once finished, cut off the homework task to take home with you for further practice.

Extension

Create a timeline that charts the sailing and sinking of the Titanic. Complete the task on page 59.

When finished, find out more about how the wreck of the Titanic was found.

Answers

1 pulled [regular], sank [irregular]

2 Regular: filled, directed
Irregular: was, were, said

3 You were not allowed to cry.
We use were for both the singular and plural form of you.

Homework

- 11:40pm – April 14th, 1912
- 12:25am – He realises the ship is lost and gives the order to fill the lifeboats "women and children first"
- 12:55am – Lifeboat #7
- 02:20am

Remember...
When something that happened in the past is finished, we use the **simple past**. We show this by changing the spelling of the verb in two ways: **regular**: +ed, +d, +ied or **irregular**: when the past tense spelling of the verb is spelt differently.

Past Simple II

> **Eight year old Marshall Drew, travelling with his Aunt and Uncle aboard the Titanic, April 14th, 1912.**
>
> When the Titanic struck the iceberg, I was in bed. However, for whatever reason I was awake and remember the jolt and cessation of motion. A steward knocked on the stateroom door and directed us to get dressed, put on life preservers and go to the boat deck, which we did.
>
> The steward, as we passed, was trying to arouse passengers who had locked themselves in for the night. Elevators were not running. We walked up to the boat deck. All was calm and orderly.
>
> An officer was in charge. "Women and children first," he said, as he directed lifeboat number eleven to be filled. There were many tearful farewells. We and Uncle Jim said good bye.
>
> The lowering of the lifeboat seventy feet to the sea was perilous. Davits, ropes, nothing worked properly, so that first one end of the lifeboat was tilted up and then down. I think it was the only time I was scared.
>
> Lifeboats pulled some distance away from the sinking Titanic, afraid of what the suction might do as row by row the porthole lights of the Titanic sank into the sea.
>
> When the Titanic upended to sink, all was blacked out until the tons of machinery crashed to the bow. As this happened hundreds and hundreds of people were thrown into the sea. It isn't likely I shall ever forget the screams of these people as they perished in water said to be twenty eight degrees…
>
> At this point in my life I was being brought up as a typical British kid. You were not allowed to cry. You were a 'little man'. So as a cool kid I lay down in the bottom of the lifeboat and went to sleep. When I awoke it was broad daylight as we approached the Carpathia.

Look at this personal recount and answer the questions below.

1 List the two examples of the simple past used in paragraph five.

2 marks

2 List the five examples of the simple past used in paragraph three. Fill in the table below.

Regular	Irregular

2 marks

3 Which line from the final paragraph is correct? Explain why.

You was not allowed to cry. ☐   You were not allowed to cry. ☐

2 marks

TOP CLASS - Grammar - Year 3

Past Simple II

Look at the verb cards below. Use them to help you finish each sentence. Draw the sign in the box, followed by the correct verb in the simple past. Which verbs are regular? Colour these yellow. Which are irregular? Colour these blue. When done, use the same verbs to create different sentences of your own.

Journey into the Past

hear

phone

1. Last night, we ☐ _____ a scary film.

2. Yesterday, dad ☐ _____ our car for £100.

watch

marry

3. We ☐ _____ lots of water because it was hot.

4. I ☐ _____ 999 after the accident.

5. The car ☐ _____ at the red light.

stop

write

6. We ☐ _____ a loud bang downstairs.

7. My sister got ☐ _____ last year.

sell

drink

8. On holiday, I ☐ _____ a postcard to my grandma.

Homework

Read about the sinking of the Titanic.
* At what time did the ship hit an iceberg?
* When did Captain Smith know the ship would sink?
* At what time was the first lifeboat launched?
* At what time did the ship sink?

Past Simple II

You are following the story of the Titanic. Create a timeline of her first and only voyage. From where did she set sail and when? Where was she heading? How long had she been sailing when she struck an iceberg? Did she sink straight away? How long did it take? What happened to the ship and its passengers during this time? When was it rediscovered?

Name: **Date:**

The Titanic – A Timeline

BUILT:

REDISCOVERED:

The Past Perfect

Think about...
Look at these characters:
Dorothy   Toto   The Scarecrow
The Cowardly Lion   The Tin Man
Which book are they from? Who wrote this story?
Is this story a book, a film or both? Which came first?

Guided

You are reading the opening chapter of the children's classic: The Wizard of Oz.

Dorothy is an orphan being looked after by her elderly Aunt Em and Uncle Henry on a farm far away. How do you think she feels? Why? Who might her best friend be? Why might she want to leave the farm? How might she do this? Where might she like to go? Why? Who might go with her?

Once done, answer the questions on page 61.

Independent

You are considering the difference between the simple past and the perfect tense.

On your own, with a partner or in a small group; complete the task sheet provided to you by your teacher on page 62.

Once finished, cut off the homework task to take home with you for further practice.

Extension

Imagine you are Toto. Complete the task on page 63.

When finished, write up your story and read it to a talk partner.

Answers

1 had baked
    had burned

2 had changed
    had taken

3 had lived
    had been

Homework

- 17th May, 1900 (USA)
- Lyman Frank Baum
- William Wallace Denslow
- Fourteen, of which *The Wonderful Wizard of Oz* was the first and most successful.

Remember...
The **past perfect** is used to talk about an action that was finished in the past. The word '**had**' comes before the verb. For example: The heat of the sun **had baked** the soil and **had turned** it grey. It **had taken** away the sparkle from Aunt Em's eyes too.

The Past Perfect

THE WIZARD OF OZ
Chapter One – The Cyclone

The sun had baked the ploughed land into a grey mass, with little cracks running through it. Even the grass was not green, for the sun had burned the tops of the long blades until they were the same grey colour to be seen everywhere. Once the house had been painted, but the sun blistered the paint and the rains washed it away, and now the house was as dull and grey as everything else.

When Aunt Em came there to live she was a young, pretty wife. The sun and wind had changed her, too. They had taken the sparkle from her eyes and left them a sober grey; they had taken the red from her cheeks and lips, and they were grey also. She was thin and gaunt, and never smiled now. When Dorothy, who was an orphan, first came to her, Aunt Em had been so startled by the child's laughter that she would scream and press her hand upon her heart whenever Dorothy's merry voice reached her ears; and she still looked at the little girl with wonder that she could find anything to laugh at.

Uncle Henry never laughed. He worked hard from morning till night and did not know what joy was. He was grey also, from his long beard to his rough boots, and he looked stern and solemn, and rarely spoke.

It was Toto that made Dorothy laugh, and saved her from growing as grey as her other surroundings. Toto was not grey; he was a little black dog, with long silky hair and small black eyes that twinkled merrily on either side of his funny, wee nose. Toto played all day long, and Dorothy played with him, and loved him dearly.

Today, however, they were not playing. Uncle Henry sat upon the doorstep and looked anxiously at the sky, which was even greyer than usual. Dorothy stood in the door with Toto in her arms, and looked at the sky too. Aunt Em was washing the dishes.

From the far north they heard a low wail of the wind, and Uncle Henry and Dorothy could see where the long grass bowed in waves before the coming storm. There now came a sharp whistling in the air from the south, and as they turned their eyes that way they saw ripples in the grass coming from that direction also.

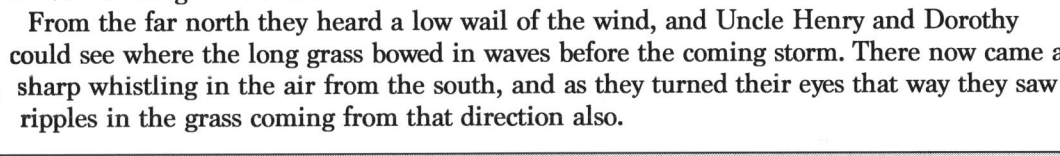

Look at this children's classic and answer the questions below.

1 Read paragraph one to complete the sentence.

The sun _____ the land and _____ the tops off the long blades of grass.

2 mark

2 Read paragraph two to complete the sentence.

The sun and the wind _____ Aunt Em too and _____ the sparkle from her eyes.

2 marks

3 Fill in the gaps to complete the sentence in your own words.

Dorothy _____ with Uncle Henry and Aunt Em for a long time. Toto, however, _____ her best friend for only a few months.

2 marks

The Past Perfect

You are looking at how to answer questions about the past. Sometimes we can use the Past Simple tense, but sometimes we need to use the Past Perfect. Answer each question using the correct tense by changing the verb in brackets.

What Happened?

Question	Verb	Simple Past	Past Perfect
Why did you get lost?	forget	I _____ the map.	I _____ the map.
Why didn't she play football?	break	She _____ her leg the day before.	She _____ her leg the day before.
Why didn't you call me?	run	My battery _____ out.	My battery _____ out.
Why was your face so red?	fall	I _____ asleep on the beach.	I _____ asleep on the beach.
Why were you late for school?	blow	The wind _____ a tree over, blocking the road.	The wind _____ a tree over, blocking the road.
Why didn't you have your dinner?	eat	I _____ a big breakfast at 11 o'clock.	I _____ a big breakfast at 11 o'clock.

Homework

Read about the book *The Wonderful Wizard of Oz*.
* When was this children's book first published?
* Who wrote this book?
* Who first illustrated this book?
* How many books appear in the Oz series?

The Past Perfect

How do you think Toto and Dorothy first met? Why might Uncle Henry and Aunt Em have brought Toto to the farm to give to Dorothy? When might they have done this? How might they have surprised her? Tell this story through the eyes of Toto.

Name: **Date:**

It's hard for a little girl to grow up far away from her friends without a mum and dad. It's hard for an uncle and an aunt to see their niece so sad and lonely.

Uncle Henry and Aunt Em knew that living on a farm in Kansas was not the most exciting place to be. So, after Dorothy had gone to bed, a plan was hatched and the very next morning Uncle Henry was on his way to pick me up.

Notes: